The Teenag Holistic Wellness Handbook

Embracing Herbs, Self-Care, and Mindfulness for a Thriving and Balanced Teen Life

Lizzie Black

The Teenage Girl's Holistic Wellness Handbook

TABLE OF CONTENTS

Chapter 1: Introduction to Holistic Wellness

In the journey of life, the teenage years are a remarkable and transformative phase. It's a period of self-discovery, growth, and the formation of values and habits that will shape your future. This chapter marks the beginning of our exploration into holistic wellness, an approach that can empower you, as a teenage girl, to blossom naturally into a balanced, healthy, and confident individual.

What Is Holistic Wellness?

Holistic wellness is a concept that transcends mere physical health. It is an all-encompassing approach that considers the interconnection between your body, mind, emotions, and spirit. Holistic wellness seeks to balance and optimize each of these dimensions, recognizing that your overall well-being is a product of their harmony. It's about looking at the bigger picture and acknowledging that good health extends beyond the absence of illness.

In the context of your teenage years, holistic wellness acknowledges that your well-being isn't solely dependent on your physical health. It also encompasses your mental and emotional health, the quality of your relationships, and your connection to the world around you. It's about nurturing a sense of purpose, self-esteem, and resilience, while also paying attention to the basics of nutrition, exercise, and sleep.

To achieve holistic wellness, you need to develop a deeper understanding of yourself, your needs, and your desires. It's about recognizing your values and aligning your life with them. Holistic wellness encourages you to be mindful of your thoughts, emotions, and actions. It's about making choices that promote health and happiness, not just for today, but for the long term.

Understanding Your Teenage Years

The teenage years are a time of profound change and exploration. You're navigating the often tumultuous waters of adolescence, experiencing physical and emotional changes, and facing new challenges and opportunities. It's a time when you begin to establish your identity, separate from your family, and build your independence. While this period can be incredibly exciting, it can also be overwhelming and confusing.

Your body is undergoing significant transformations during adolescence. Hormones surge, leading to the development of secondary sexual characteristics and the beginning of the menstrual cycle for many girls. These hormonal changes can influence your emotions, your energy levels, and even your skin. As a result, it's common to experience mood swings, acne, and sometimes discomfort. Understanding these changes is the first step in accepting them and learning how to manage them effectively.

Emotionally, you're exploring your own beliefs, values, and principles. You're seeking to define who you are and what you want out of life. Peer pressure, academic demands, and the desire to fit in can sometimes lead to stress and anxiety. But it' important to know that these emotions are a natura part of growing up. They are the raw materials fron which you will build resilience, empathy, an self-awareness.

Benefits of a Holistic Approach

Embracing holistic wellness as a teenager offer numerous benefits. First and foremost, it empower you to take charge of your health and well-being. B considering your physical, mental, emotional, an spiritual aspects, you create a more comprehensiv and resilient foundation for a healthy future.

This approach helps you build self-awareness. By examining your feelings, thoughts, and behavior from a holistic perspective, you gain a deepe understanding of yourself. You'll learn to recogniz the triggers for stress and anxiety and develop strategies for managing them. You'll also discover your strengths and weaknesses, which can guide your choices and goals.

Holistic wellness encourages you to build strong relationships. It emphasizes the importance of open communication and empathy. By learning to understand and connect with others on a deeper level, you can foster more meaningful and supportive relationships with your family, friends, and potential romantic partners.

Another significant benefit of holistic wellness is the development of resilience and coping skills. Life is full of challenges, and your teenage years are no exception. A holistic approach equips you with the tools to bounce back from setbacks and face adversity with courage and determination. It's abou learning to adapt to change and use it as ar opportunity for growth.

Finally, holistic wellness nurtures your self-esteem and confidence. By valuing all aspects of your being and setting goals that align with your values, you'l develop a strong sense of self-worth. This, in turn empowers you to make choices that are in your bes interest, rather than succumbing to externa pressures.

As we delve deeper into the holistic wellness journey each subsequent chapter will provide you with practical tips and guidance to support your growth and well-being during your teenage years. By embracing holistic wellness, you'll be better equipped to navigate the challenges and seize the opportunities that come your way, allowing you tc blossom naturally into the incredible individual you are meant to be.

Chapter 2: Mindful Self-Care

In our fast-paced, modern world, the concept of self-care has become increasingly important. For teenage girls, the need for self-care is especially crucial, as you navigate the challenges and opportunities of adolescence. This chapter explores the significance of self-care, the impact of mindfulness, and how to craft a self-care routine tailored to your unique needs.

The Importance of Self-Care

Self-care, at its core, is about taking deliberate actions to preserve and improve your well-being. It is a proactive approach to maintaining a balance between your physical, mental, and emotional health. Self-care is not a luxury; it is a necessity, especially in a time when external pressures and expectations can weigh heavily on your shoulders.

For teenage girls, self-care is an essential part of nurturing a healthy relationship with yourself. It is a practice that promotes self-compassion, self-love, and self-acceptance. By making self-care a priority, you send a powerful message to yourself that you are worthy of care and attention.

Self-care is not a one-size-fits-all concept. It looks different for each person and may include activities like reading, drawing, taking a bubble bath, spending time with friends, or simply taking a quiet moment to breathe and reflect. It can be as simple as maintaining good hygiene and getting enough sleep, or as complex as setting boundaries and making time for your passions.

In the midst of the hustle and bustle of teenage life self-care acts as a reset button. It allows you to step away from your daily challenges and stressors offering a chance to relax, recharge, and regain perspective. By practicing self-care, you build a strong foundation for your holistic wellness, ensuring that you are better equipped to face the demands of adolescence.

Mindfulness and Its Impact

Mindfulness is an integral part of self-care, offering a powerful tool to help you stay present and fully engaged in your life. In essence, mindfulness is the practice of paying attention to the present momen without judgment. It encourages you to observe you thoughts, emotions, and sensations as they arise promoting a deeper understanding of yourself.

For teenage girls, mindfulness can be a game-changer. The teenage years are often marked by an overabundance of worries about the future and regrets about the past. Mindfulness helps you break free from these patterns and allows you to experience life as it unfolds in the here and now.

The impact of mindfulness on your well-being is profound. It can reduce stress, anxiety, and symptoms of depression. By bringing your attention to the present, you can break the cycle of rumination, which often fuels negative emotions. Mindfulness also promotes emotional regulation, helping you respond to situations with greater awareness and less reactivity.

In the context of self-care, mindfulness enhances the quality of your self-care activities. When you engage in self-care mindfully, you savor every moment and experience it more deeply. Whether you're taking a nature walk, sipping a cup of herbal tea, or meditating, mindfulness allows you to be fully present and appreciate the simple joys of life.

Crafting Your Self-Care Routine

Creating a self-care routine tailored to your needs is a powerful act of self-compassion. It's a commitment to your well-being and an acknowledgment that you deserve time and care. Craft a self-care routine that is both meaningful and sustainable for you. Here are some steps to help you get started:

Identify Your Needs: The first step in crafting a self-care routine is to recognize your needs. What makes you feel relaxed, recharged, and joyful? Is it spending time with friends, reading a book, doing yoga, or simply taking a few minutes to breathe deeply? Identify the activities and practices that resonate with you.

Set Priorities: In your busy life, you may have many responsibilities. It's crucial to prioritize self-care. Make a list of self-care activities that you find most beneficial and prioritize them. Understand that self-care is not selfish; it's a necessary part of maintaining your well-being.

Create a Schedule: To make self-care a habit, schedule it into your daily or weekly routine. Set aside dedicated time for self-care activities. This can be in the morning, during a lunch break, or before bedtime, depending on your preferences and availability.

Set Boundaries: Learn to say no when needed. Setting boundaries is an essential aspect of self-care. It's okay to decline invitations or requests that may drain your energy or time that you've allocated for self-care.

Practice Mindfulness: Incorporate mindfulness into your self-care routine. Engage in self-care activities with full presence and awareness. Whether you're taking a bath, enjoying a hobby, or savoring a meal, do it mindfully.

Experiment and Adapt: Self-care is a personal journey, and what works for one person may not work for another. Be open to experimentation and adaptation. If you try a self-care activity and it doesn't resonate with you, don't be discouraged; explore other options until you find what truly nourishes you.

Stay Consistent: Consistency is key in self-care. Regular self-care practices provide ongoing benefits.

If you fall off track, don't be too hard on yourself; simply return to your routine with kindness and commitment.

Seek Support: Share your self-care journey with trusted friends, family members, or mentors. They can offer guidance and encouragement, and you can even engage in self-care activities together.

Remember that your self-care routine is a reflection of your self-worth and self-love. By embracing self-care and mindfulness as a part of your holistic wellness journey, you not only take better care of yourself but also set a positive example for others. Self-care is an investment in your physical, mental, and emotional well-being, and it empowers you to navigate the challenges of your teenage years with grace and resilience.

Chapter 3: Nourishing Your Body

Nourishing your body is a cornerstone of holisti
wellness, and it's especially vital during your teenag
years. This chapter delves into the importance o
nutrition for teenage girls, the role of hydration, an
the exploration of nutrient-rich foods, equipping yo
with the knowledge to make informed and nourishin
choices for your well-being.

Nutrition for Teenage Girls

During adolescence, your body undergoes significan
growth and development, which places uniqu
nutritional demands on you. Proper nutrition i
essential to support physical growth, brai

development, and hormonal changes. Here are some key aspects of nutrition for teenage girls:

Balanced Diet: A balanced diet provides the necessary nutrients for growth and overall well-being. Include a variety of food groups in your meals, such as fruits, vegetables, whole grains, lean proteins, and dairy products or dairy alternatives.

Iron and Calcium: Iron is vital for energy and brain function, while calcium supports bone health. Teenage girls often need more of these nutrients due to growth spurts and menstrual losses. Good sources of iron include lean meats, legumes, and fortified cereals. Calcium can be found in dairy products, leafy greens, and fortified non-dairy alternatives.

Protein: Protein is crucial for muscle development and overall health. Include sources of protein like lean meats, poultry, fish, beans, and tofu in your diet.

Fiber: Fiber aids in digestion and helps maintain a healthy weight. Incorporate whole grains, fruits, and vegetables to increase your fiber intake.

Hydration: Proper hydration is key for optimal bodily functions. Drink water throughout the day and consider consuming foods with high water content like fruits and vegetables.

Avoid Sugary and Processed Foods: While it's okay to enjoy treats occasionally, limit your consumption of sugary and processed foods. These can provide empty calories and little nutritional value.

Portion Control: Pay attention to portion sizes. Eating the right portions can help you maintain a healthy weight and avoid overeating.

Listen to Your Body: Pay attention to your body's hunger and fullness cues. Eat when you're hungry and stop when you're satisfied.

Eat Mindfully: Practice mindful eating, which involves savoring each bite and being present during meals

This can help prevent overeating and promote a healthier relationship with food.

Remember, everyone's nutritional needs are different, and it's essential to consult with a healthcare professional or registered dietitian for personalized guidance. They can help you create a meal plan that aligns with your specific needs and preferences.

The Role of Hydration

Water is the elixir of life, and adequate hydration is crucial for your overall well-being. Your body is composed of approximately 60% water, and it plays vital roles in various bodily functions:

Temperature Regulation: Water helps maintain your body's temperature within a narrow range. This is particularly important when you engage in physica activities or are exposed to extreme temperatures.

Digestion and Nutrient Absorption: Water aids in the digestion of food and the absorption of nutrients ir the gastrointestinal tract.

Circulation: Blood, which carries oxygen and nutrients to your cells, is primarily composed of water. Prope hydration ensures that your circulatory systerr functions optimally.

Detoxification: Water helps eliminate waste products and toxins from your body through urine, sweat, and other bodily fluids.

Joint Lubrication: Adequate hydration keeps your joints well-lubricated and may prevent discomfort and pain.

For teenage girls, maintaining proper hydration is essential. Dehydration can lead to a range of health issues, including fatigue, headaches, and difficulty concentrating. It can also affect physical performance, mood, and overall well-being.

So, how can you ensure you stay adequately hydrated? Here are some tips:

Drink Water Regularly: Make it a habit to drink water throughout the day, even if you're not particularly thirsty. Carry a reusable water bottle to remind yourself to hydrate.

Monitor Urine Color: Your urine color can be an indicator of your hydration status. Pale yellow or light straw-colored urine is a good sign, while dark yellow or amber-colored urine may indicate dehydration.

Consider Electrolytes: If you engage in strenuous physical activity or sweat heavily, you may need to replace electrolytes lost through sweat. Sports drinks or foods like bananas and oranges can help.

Pay Attention to Your Body: Thirst is a clear signa that your body needs hydration. Listen to your bod and drink water when you're thirsty.

Limit Sugary and Caffeinated Drinks: While it's okay t enjoy these beverages in moderation, they shoul not be your primary source of hydration. Wate should be your go-to choice.

Exploring Nutrient-Rich Foods

Exploring nutrient-rich foods is an exciting journe that can enhance your overall well-being and set th stage for a lifetime of healthy eating. Nutrient-ric foods are those that provide a high concentration o essential vitamins, minerals, and other beneficia compounds relative to their calorie content.

Here are some nutrient-rich foods you can include i your diet:

Fruits and Vegetables: These are packed with vitamins, minerals, and antioxidants that support your immune system, skin health, and overall vitality. Try to incorporate a variety of colorful fruits and vegetables into your meals.

Whole Grains: Whole grains, such as whole wheat, brown rice, quinoa, and oats, provide fiber and complex carbohydrates that offer sustained energy and promote digestive health.

Lean Proteins: Lean sources of protein, like skinless poultry, fish, tofu, and legumes, are essential for muscle growth and repair. They also keep you feeling full and satisfied.

Dairy or Dairy Alternatives: These are rich in calcium and vitamin D, which support bone health. Choose low-fat or non-fat options if you're concerned about calories.

Nuts and Seeds: These are excellent sources of healthy fats, vitamins, minerals, and protein. They make for satisfying snacks or additions to meals.

Fish: Fatty fish like salmon, mackerel, and trout are rich in omega-3 fatty acids, which support heart and brain health.

Herbs and Spices: Many herbs and spices offer antioxidant and anti-inflammatory properties. They can add flavor and health benefits to your meals.

When exploring nutrient-rich foods, aim for variety and balance in your diet. Try new foods and recipes to keep your meals exciting and nutritious. Also, be mindful of portion sizes to ensure that you are meeting your nutritional needs without overeating.

By nourishing your body with a well-balanced diet, staying adequately hydrated, and exploring nutrient-rich foods, you are setting a strong foundation for your holistic wellness journey. Your teenage years are a time of growth and discovery, and the way you fuel your body plays a vital role in your physical and emotional well-being. Embrace these principles of nourishment, and you'll be well on your way to blossoming naturally into a healthier, happier, and more confident young woman.

Chapter 4: Embracing Physical Well-Being

Physical well-being is an essential aspect of holistic wellness. Your body and mind are intricately connected, and nurturing your physical health can have a profound impact on your overall well-being. In this chapter, we explore the significance of exercise and its mental health benefits, finding an exercise routine you love, and the holistic benefits of yoga.

Exercise and Its Mental Health Benefits

Exercise is not just about maintaining a healthy body; it also plays a crucial role in supporting your mental health. The teenage years can be a time of heightened stress and emotional turbulence, and exercise can be a valuable tool in managing these challenges.

Here are some of the mental health benefits of exercise:

Stress Reduction: Exercise is a powerful stress reliever. It helps your body release endorphins, which are natural mood lifters. Physical activity can help you unwind, reduce tension, and provide a healthy escape from the pressures of teenage life.

Anxiety Management: Regular exercise can reduce symptoms of anxiety. It promotes relaxation and can help you cope with anxiety-related disorders, such as generalized anxiety disorder and social anxiety.

Improved Mood: Exercise has a direct impact o
mood regulation. It can enhance your overall sense o
well-being, boost self-esteem, and improve bod
image.

Enhanced Cognitive Function: Exercise has bee
shown to improve cognitive function, includin
memory and concentration. This can be particularl
beneficial for academic performance during you
teenage years.

Better Sleep: Physical activity can lead to more restfu
sleep. A good night's sleep is crucial for emotiona
regulation and mental clarity.

Increased Resilience: Regular exercise builds physica
and mental resilience. It teaches you to push throug
challenges, which can translate to improve

emotional resilience when dealing with life's ups and downs.

Finding the exercise routine that suits you is key to reaping these mental health benefits. It should be something you enjoy and look forward to rather than a chore.

Finding an Exercise Routine You Love

Discovering an exercise routine you love is the secret to consistent physical activity. Here are some tips to help you find the right fit:

Explore Your Interests: Start by exploring activities that genuinely interest you. Do you enjoy dancing, swimming, hiking, or team sports? The more you enjoy an activity, the more likely you are to stick with it.

Try Different Activities: Don't be afraid to try a variety of activities to find what resonates with you. You might be surprised by what you enjoy once you give it a chance.

Consider Your Personality: Your exercise routine should align with your personality. If you're a social butterfly, group classes or team sports might be appealing. If you're more introverted, solo activities like hiking or yoga might be a better fit.

Set Realistic Goals: Set achievable goals for yourself. This could be completing a 5K run, being able to perform a certain yoga pose, or simply maintaining a regular exercise routine.

Make It Fun: Exercise doesn't have to be a serious endeavor. Incorporate fun elements into your routine, whether it's dancing to your favorite music or playing a sport with friends.

Mix It Up: Variety can keep your routine exciting. Alternate between different activities to prevent boredom and overuse injuries.

Seek Support: Share your fitness journey with friends or family. Having an exercise buddy can make the experience more enjoyable and provide mutual motivation.

Embrace Mindfulness: Exercise can also be an opportunity to practice mindfulness. Pay attention to the sensations in your body, the rhythm of your breath, and the environment around you. This can deepen your connection to your physical well-being.

Remember that the most important factor is consistency. It's better to do a physical activity you enjoy regularly than to do something you dislike sporadically. Your exercise routine should become a part of your lifestyle, not a temporary fix.

Yoga and Its Holistic Benefits

Yoga is a unique form of exercise that goes beyond physical fitness. It is a holistic practice that nurtures your body, mind, and spirit. Here's why yoga can be a valuable addition to your holistic wellness journey:

Physical Benefits: Yoga enhances flexibility, strength, and balance. It can improve posture and reduce the risk of injury. Its low-impact nature makes it suitable for people of all fitness levels.

Stress Reduction: Yoga incorporates deep breathing and mindfulness, which are effective stress reduction techniques. The practice encourages relaxation and the release of physical and mental tension.

Emotional Well-Being: Yoga helps you connect with your emotions and improve emotional regulation. It provides a safe space for self-reflection and self-compassion.

Mental Clarity: The mindfulness practiced in yoga can sharpen your mental focus and improve cognitive function. This can be particularly beneficial for academic and creative pursuits.

Self-Awareness: Yoga encourages self-awareness, self-acceptance, and self-compassion. It's a journey of self-discovery that fosters a positive relationship with your body.

Balance and Harmony: Yoga aims to create a sense of balance and harmony within. It teaches you to live in the present moment, accept change, and find equanimity in challenging situations.

Spiritual Connection: For some, yoga is a spiritual practice that connects them to a higher sense of purpose or spirituality. It can provide a sense of peace and purpose in life.

To get started with yoga, you don't need to be a contortionist or a guru. There are many styles of yoga, from vigorous vinyasa to gentle hatha, and you can find classes or online resources tailored to your level and interests. Even a few minutes of daily practice can make a significant difference in your physical and mental well-being.

Incorporating exercise, especially an activity you love, into your daily routine, and exploring the holistic benefits of yoga can have a transformative impact on your physical well-being and mental health. These practices can help you navigate the challenges and opportunities of your teenage years with resilience, self-assurance, and a holistic approach to wellness.

Chapter 5: Managing Stress and Anxiety

The teenage years can be both exciting and challenging, marked by new experiences, friendships, and academic responsibilities. However, they can also bring about stress and anxiety as you navigate various life changes. In this chapter, we explore the importance of identifying stressors, stress-relief techniques tailored for teens, and strategies to cope with anxiety and the pressures of school.

Identifying Stressors

Understanding the sources of your stress is the first step in managing it effectively. Stressors can be categorized into several areas, including:

Academic Stress: The pressure to perform well in school, manage deadlines, and excel in exams can be a significant source of stress for many teens.

Social Stress: Friendships, peer pressure, and the desire to fit in can lead to social stress. It's common to worry about acceptance, rejection, or conflicts with peers.

Family Stress: Family dynamics, conflicts, and high expectations from parents or caregivers can contribute to stress.

Personal Stress: Personal stressors can include body image concerns, self-esteem issues, and the desire to achieve personal goals.

Extracurricular Stress: Involvement in extracurricular activities, sports, or part-time jobs can add to your stress load.

Global and Environmental Stress: The state of the world, concerns about the environment, or global issues can also weigh on your mind.

Health Stress: Physical health issues, illness, or worries about your health or that of loved ones can be sources of stress.

It's important to recognize that stress is a natural response to challenging situations, and it can even be beneficial in small doses, motivating you to accomplish tasks and overcome obstacles. However, chronic or excessive stress can lead to physical and mental health problems. By identifying the specific stressors in your life, you can take steps to address them and reduce their impact.

Stress-Relief Techniques for Teens

Managing stress and anxiety is essential for your well-being. Fortunately, there are several stress-relief techniques tailored for teens that can help you cope with the challenges of adolescence:

Deep Breathing: Practice deep, diaphragmatic breathing to calm your nervous system. Inhale deeply through your nose, hold for a few seconds, and then exhale slowly through your mouth.

Mindfulness Meditation: Incorporate mindfulness meditation into your routine. It can help you stay present and reduce anxiety. Apps and online resources offer guided sessions.

Exercise: Regular physical activity releases endorphins, the body's natural mood lifters. Engage in activities you enjoy, whether it's dancing, jogging, or practicing yoga.

Journaling: Keep a journal to express your thoughts and emotions. Writing can help you process your feelings and gain clarity.

Talk to a Trusted Adult: Share your concerns with a trusted adult, whether it's a parent, teacher, counselor, or family friend. They can offer guidance and support.

Connect with Friends: Spending time with friends and loved ones can provide emotional support and a sense of belonging. Sharing your thoughts and feelings with trusted friends can be cathartic.

Time Management: Organize your schedule and prioritize tasks to manage academic and extracurricular responsibilities effectively.

Set Realistic Goals: Be realistic in setting goals for yourself. Break larger goals into smaller, manageable steps to reduce feelings of overwhelm.

Limit Screen Time: Reduce screen time, especially before bedtime, to ensure better sleep and a calmer mind.

Creative Outlets: Engage in creative activities that bring joy and allow self-expression, whether it's art, music, writing, or other hobbies.

Relaxation Techniques: Practice relaxation techniques like progressive muscle relaxation or guided imagery to unwind and relieve tension.

Seek Professional Help: If you're struggling with persistent stress or anxiety, don't hesitate to seek the support of a mental health professional or counselor.

Coping with Anxiety and School Pressures

Coping with anxiety, especially in the face of school pressures, is a significant concern for many teens. Here are some strategies to help you manage anxiety effectively:

Time Management: Create a study schedule and allocate dedicated time for homework and test preparation. This can prevent last-minute cramming and reduce anxiety.

Break Tasks into Smaller Steps: Divide assignments into smaller, manageable tasks. Tackling one step at a time can make the workload feel less overwhelming.

Healthy Lifestyle: Prioritize good sleep, a balanced diet, and regular exercise. These factors contribute to a healthier mind and body, which can better handle stress.

Breathing Exercises: When anxiety strikes, use deep breathing techniques to calm your nerves. Take a moment to inhale deeply and exhale slowly.

Mindfulness and Relaxation: Incorporate mindfulness and relaxation practices into your routine to reduce overall stress and anxiety.

Positive Self-Talk: Challenge negative self-talk and replace it with positive affirmations. Believe in your capabilities and strengths.

Study Groups: Collaborate with peers in study groups. Discussing and learning together can ease academic stress.

Seek Support: If you're struggling with anxiety, seek support from a counselor or therapist. Cognitive-behavioral therapy (CBT) is an effective approach for managing anxiety.

Remember that managing stress and anxiety is an ongoing process, and it's perfectly normal to experience moments of stress during your teenage years. By identifying stressors, practicing stress-relief techniques tailored for teens, and implementing coping strategies, you can build resilience and face the challenges of adolescence with greater confidence and well-being.

Chapter 6: Building Healthy Relationships

As you journey through your teenage years, building and maintaining healthy relationships becomes a significant part of your holistic wellness. This chapter delves into the dynamics of family relationships and communication, navigating friendships and peer pressure, and developing positive romantic relationships. Healthy relationships are a vital aspect of your overall well-being, influencing your mental and emotional health.

Family Dynamics and Communication

Your family is a cornerstone of your life, and the dynamics within your family play a substantial role in your development and well-being. Here are some key aspects to consider when it comes to family dynamics and communication:

Open and Honest Communication: Effective communication is at the heart of a healthy family dynamic. Encourage open and honest conversations with your family members. Share your thoughts and feelings, and be an active listener as well. By fostering good communication, you can better understand each other and build stronger bonds.

Boundaries: Establishing healthy boundaries within the family is crucial. Respect each other's personal space and privacy. Discuss and agree on rules and expectations to create a harmonious environment.

Conflict Resolution: Conflicts are a natural part of any family dynamic. Learn how to resolve conflicts in a constructive and respectful manner. Use "I"

statements to express your feelings and avoid blame
Seek compromise and common ground.

Quality Time: Make an effort to spend quality time with your family. This can be as simple as sharing a meal, playing games, or engaging in activities you all enjoy. Quality time strengthens the emotional bonds within the family.

Support System: Your family is your primary support system. Share your goals, dreams, and challenges with them. In turn, be supportive of their aspirations and challenges. A supportive family environment can bolster your self-esteem and resilience.

Respect and Empathy: Treat each other with respect and empathy. Understand that every family member has their own experiences, feelings, and perspectives Empathizing with each other's struggles and triumphs can create a deeper connection.

Roles and Responsibilities: Acknowledge and share roles and responsibilities within the family. This can include chores, tasks, and caregiving. A fair distribution of responsibilities fosters cooperation and a sense of fairness.

Independence and Autonomy: As you grow into adolescence, you seek more independence and autonomy. It's natural to want to make your own decisions and assert your individuality. Communicate your needs for independence with respect and consideration.

Family Traditions and Rituals: Establish and maintain family traditions and rituals. These traditions can create a sense of continuity and connection, which is especially important during times of change.

Navigating family dynamics and communication can be challenging, but it's a significant step toward maintaining a healthy and supportive environment. A strong family foundation contributes to your overall well-being and equips you with the skills to build positive relationships outside the family.

Navigating Friendships and Peer Pressure

Friendships play a pivotal role in your teenage years. They provide companionship, emotional support, and a sense of belonging. However, peer pressure can also be a significant influence. Here are some tips for navigating friendships and managing peer pressure:

Choosing Friends: Be selective about the friends you choose. Surround yourself with individuals who share your values and uplift your well-being. Healthy friendships are built on trust, mutual respect, and support.

Communication: Effective communication is as important in friendships as it is in family relationships. Discuss your feelings, expectations, and boundaries with your friends. Encourage open and honest conversations.

Empathy and Understanding: Cultivate empathy and understanding in your friendships. Recognize and validate your friends' feelings and experiences. This fosters trust and emotional connection.

Boundaries: Set healthy boundaries in your friendships. It's important to assert your values and limits, even when your friends have different preferences. Respect each other's boundaries and autonomy.

Peer Pressure: Peer pressure is a common challenge in adolescence. Be aware of the influence of peer pressure and stand firm in your values and decisions. It's okay to say no when you're uncomfortable with a particular situation.

Conflict Resolution: Conflicts can arise in friendships. Use effective conflict resolution skills, such as active listening and compromise, to address conflicts in a constructive manner.

Loyalty and Trust: Loyalty and trust are vital in friendships. Be a reliable and trustworthy friend, and expect the same in return. Building trust takes time and consistency.

Quality Over Quantity: It's not about the quantity of friends but the quality of friendships. Focus on maintaining a few close, meaningful connections rather than pursuing popularity.

Support and Encouragement: Offer support and encouragement to your friends. Celebrate their successes and provide a listening ear during their challenges. Healthy friendships involve mutual support.

Independence: While friendships are essential, maintain your independence. Don't rely solely on friends for validation or self-worth. Develop a healthy sense of self-esteem and self-reliance.

Navigating friendships during your teenage years is an opportunity for personal growth and self-discovery. Healthy friendships can provide valuable support and enrich your life. Remember that quality and authenticity are more important than quantity.

Developing Positive Romantic Relationships

As you grow into adolescence, you may start exploring romantic relationships. Developing positive romantic relationships involves understanding your own needs and desires and respecting the needs and boundaries of your partner. Here are some key aspects to consider:

Self-Awareness: Before entering a romantic relationship, take time to understand yourself. What are your values, interests, and goals? Knowing yourself well can guide you in choosing a compatible partner.

Respect: Respect is the foundation of any healthy relationship. Treat your partner with respect and expect the same in return. This includes respecting boundaries, consent, and personal space.

Communication: Effective communication is essential in romantic relationships. Be open and honest with your partner about your feelings, concerns, and expectations. Listening to your partner with empathy is equally important.

Boundaries: Establish clear boundaries in your romantic relationship. These boundaries should be mutually agreed upon and respected. Boundaries can pertain to physical intimacy, time spent together, and individual needs.

Mutual Interests and Goals: Shared interests and goals can strengthen a romantic relationship. They provide common ground for activities and aspirations.

Healthy Conflict Resolution: Conflicts are a part of any relationship. Learn to address conflicts in a constructive and respectful manner. Avoid blame and focus on finding solutions together.

Independence: While romantic relationships are important, it's crucial to maintain your independence. Continue to nurture your friendships, pursue personal interests, and focus on self-development.

Trust and Loyalty: Trust and loyalty are the cornerstones of a healthy romantic relationship. Build trust through honesty and reliability. Maintain loyalty and commitment to each other.

Consent: Consent is a fundamental aspect of any physical aspect of a romantic relationship. Always seek and respect your partner's consent and communicate openly about physical boundaries.

Self-Care: Don't neglect self-care in the pursuit of a romantic relationship. Your well-being should always be a priority.

Remember that developing positive romantic relationships takes time and effort. It's essential to prioritize your own well-being and respect the well-being of your partner. Healthy relationships should enhance your life, not create stress or conflict. By building a foundation of respect, communication, and understanding, you can foster positive relationships in your teenage years and beyond.

Chapter 7: Enhancing Emotional Intelligence

Emotions are the threads that weave the intricate tapestry of our lives. They color our experiences, influence our decisions, and impact our well-being. In this chapter, we explore the facets of emotional intelligence, from understanding your emotions to developing emotional resilience and coping strategies. We also delve into the importance of practicing empathy and self-compassion to enhance your emotional well-being.

Understanding Emotions

Emotions are the language of your inner world. They provide insight into your feelings and reactions to various situations. Understanding your emotions is the first step in enhancing your emotional intelligence. Here are some key aspects to consider:

Emotion Identification: Begin by identifying and labeling your emotions. Recognize when you're feeling happy, sad, angry, anxious, or any other emotion. Journaling can be a helpful tool in this process.

Acceptance: Emotions are neither good nor bad; they simply are. Practice self-acceptance by acknowledging and accepting your emotions without judgment. It's okay to feel the way you do.

Emotional Awareness: Pay attention to the physical sensations that accompany your emotions. For example, stress might manifest as tension in your shoulders, while joy can feel like a lightness in your heart.

Triggers: Identify the situations or events that trigge specific emotions. Knowing your triggers can help yo anticipate and manage your emotional responses.

Emotional Cues: Understand the cues that signal you emotional state. These cues can include changes i your tone of voice, body language, or facia expressions.

Emotional Vocabulary: Build a rich emotiona vocabulary to describe your feelings accurately. Th more nuanced your vocabulary, the better you ca express your emotions to yourself and others.

Emotion Regulation: Learn how to regulate you emotions effectively. This involves managing intens emotions and preventing them from overwhelmin you.

Emotional intelligence is not about suppressin emotions but about recognizing and responding t them in a healthy and constructive way. The bette you understand your own emotions, the more equipped you'll be to manage them.

Emotional Resilience and Coping Strategies

Life is full of challenges, and emotional resilience is the ability to bounce back from setbacks and adapt to adversity. Developing emotional resilience is a crucial component of enhancing your emotional intelligence. Here are some strategies to build emotional resilience:

Positive Mindset: Cultivate a positive mindset by focusing on your strengths and past successes. Optimism can help you navigate challenges with greater ease.
Self-Care: Prioritize self-care to maintain your emotional well-being. This includes getting adequate

sleep, eating a balanced diet, and engaging in regula
physical activity.

Stress Reduction: Practice stress reductior techniques, such as deep breathing, meditation, or mindfulness. These strategies can help you manage and reduce stress.

Problem-Solving: Approach challenges with a problem-solving mindset. Break problems down intc manageable steps and seek solutions actively.

Social Support: Lean on your support network, including friends and family, when facing difficulties. They can offer emotional support and perspective.

Resilience Building: Accept that setbacks are a part of life and opportunities for growth. Embrace challenges as opportunities to develop resilience.

Self-Compassion: Be kind and compassionate toward yourself. Self-compassion involves treating yourself with the same care and understanding that you would offer to a friend.

Acceptance of Change: Life is constantly changing. Embrace change as a natural part of the human experience, and adapt with an open heart.

Emotional resilience is not about avoiding or suppressing negative emotions; it's about navigating them with grace and finding constructive ways to cope with life's ups and downs.

Practicing Empathy and Self-Compassion

Empathy and self-compassion are two pillars of emotional intelligence that greatly enhance your relationships and well-being.

Empathy: Empathy is the ability to understand and share the feelings of others. Practicing empathy allows you to connect more deeply with people and foster supportive relationships. To develop empathy:

Active Listening: Listen attentively to others, and ask open-ended questions to better understand their perspectives and feelings.

Perspective-Taking: Put yourself in someone else's shoes to understand their experiences and emotions.

Nonverbal Cues: Pay attention to nonverbal cues such as body language and facial expressions, to grasp the emotions behind the words.

Self-Compassion: Self-compassion is extending the same kindness, understanding, and support to yourself as you would to a friend in times of suffering. It involves:

Self-Kindness: Treat yourself with kindness and care, especially when you make mistakes or face challenges.

Common Humanity: Remember that suffering is a shared human experience. You are not alone in your struggles.

Mindfulness: Approach your emotions with mindful awareness, observing them without judgment.

Practicing empathy and self-compassion can improve your relationships, enhance your self-esteem, and boost your overall emotional well-being.

Enhancing emotional intelligence is an ongoing journey, and it's a vital skill that will benefit you throughout your life. By understanding your emotions, building emotional resilience, and practicing empathy and self-compassion, you'll develop a deep sense of self-awareness and emotional well-being, enriching your life and your connections with others.

Chapter 8: Mind-Body Connection

In the journey towards holistic well-being, one of th most fascinating and powerful aspects to explore i the profound connection between your mind an body. Your thoughts, emotions, and mental state ar intricately linked to your physical health and overa well-being. In this chapter, we'll embark on a journe to explore the mind-body link, discover the numerou benefits of meditation, and learn how to harness th incredible power of visualization to nurture you holistic wellness.

Exploring the Mind-Body Link

The mind-body connection is a captivating and age-old concept that has been recognized by numerous ancient healing traditions, including Ayurveda, Traditional Chinese Medicine, and holistic practices. It's a concept that has gained increasing recognition in modern medicine and science, revealing the significant influence our mental and emotional states have on our physical health.

Understanding the mind-body connection is a pivotal step in your journey towards holistic well-being. Here are some key insights to consider:

Stress and Physical Health: Chronic stress can take a toll on your physical well-being, leading to symptoms like headaches, muscle tension, and digestive issues. Stress hormones, particularly cortisol, can disrupt various bodily functions.

Emotions and Immune System: Emotions play a significant role in the functioning of your immune system. Negative emotions, such as anger and anxiety, can weaken the immune system, while positive emotions and a hopeful outlook can boost immunity.

Pain Perception: Your thoughts and emotions can influence your perception of pain. Managing pain often involves addressing both the emotional and physical aspects of the experience.

Healing and Recovery: A positive mindset can expedite the healing and recovery process. Believing in your body's innate capacity to heal is a powerful catalyst for the healing journey.

Long-Term Health Impact: Prolonged negative emotions and stress can contribute to the development of chronic health conditions, including heart disease, hypertension, and autoimmune disorders.

Placebo Effect: The placebo effect, where a belief in the effectiveness of a treatment leads to actual health improvements, is a testament to the power of the mind in influencing physical outcomes.

Mindful Eating: The mind-body connection extends to your eating habits. Practicing mindful eating involves being fully present during meals, which can lead to healthier food choices and improved digestion.

Understanding the intricate web of the mind-body connection underscores the significance of nurturing your mental and emotional well-being for the sake of your physical health. It emphasizes that holistic well-being encompasses the entirety of your being.

Meditation and Its Benefits

Meditation is a remarkable and transformative tool for harnessing the power of the mind-body connection. It is a practice that encourages mindfulness, cultivating a harmonious relationship between your mind and body. Let's explore the numerous benefits of meditation:

Stress Reduction: Meditation is renowned for its stress-reduction benefits. It has the power to calm the mind, lower the production of stress hormones, and induce a state of relaxation.

Emotional Regulation: Through meditation, you can enhance your capacity to manage your emotions by increasing emotional awareness. It provides a space for you to observe your feelings without judgment.

Improved Concentration: Regular meditation can boost your ability to focus and concentrate, which can significantly impact your academic and professional achievements.

Enhanced Immune Function: Meditation has been linked to an improved immune system. It can strengthen the immune response and reduce susceptibility to illnesses.

Better Sleep: A calm and centered mind promotes better sleep quality. Meditation can alleviate insomnia and improve your sleep patterns, allowing you to wake up refreshed and rejuvenated.

Pain Management: Meditation has the ability to reduce the perception of pain by altering how the brain processes pain signals. It provides an effective tool for those dealing with chronic pain conditions.

Mind-Body Connection: Meditation reinforces the connection between your mind and body by encouraging you to be fully present in the moment, to connect with your body's sensations, and to understand the signals it sends.

Emotional Resilience: Meditation can increase emotional resilience, making it easier for you to navigate life's challenges with grace and poise. It

allows you to respond to difficulties with a sense o
calm and perspective.

There are various forms of meditation, from mindfulness meditation, which involves being fully present in the moment, to loving-kindness meditation, which cultivates feelings of compassion and empathy towards yourself and others. These practices provide a wealth of benefits for you mental, emotional, and physical well-being, making them essential tools in your holistic well-being toolkit.

Harnessing the Power of Visualization

Visualization is a powerful technique that taps into the mind-body connection to create positive change in your life. It's a process of using your imagination to mentally rehearse or create vivid mental images o your goals and aspirations. Visualization is a holistic tool that has been used by athletes, artists, and individuals in various fields to enhance performance and well-being.

Here's how you can harness the power of visualization:

Set Clear Intentions: Begin by setting clear and specific intentions. What is it that you want to achieve or manifest in your life? Whether it's a specific goal, improved well-being, or enhanced self-confidence, clearly define your intention.
Create a Peaceful Space: Find a quiet and comfortable space where you won't be disturbed. Close your eyes, take a few deep breaths, and relax your body and mind.
Visualize Your Intention: In your mind's eye, vividly imagine your intention as if it has already come to

fruition. Use all your senses to create a detailed mental image. See, hear, feel, and even smell the experience.

Engage Emotionally: As you visualize, engage your emotions. Feel the joy, gratitude, and fulfillment associated with the realization of your intention. Let these positive emotions flow through you.

Be Consistent: Practice visualization regularly. It's like a mental workout for your goals and aspirations. The more you engage with the process, the more powerful it becomes.

Trust the Process: Trust that the act of visualization is a potent force that can influence your reality. Have faith in the mind-body connection and your ability to bring about positive change.

Visualization can be used for various purposes, including achieving academic success, overcoming challenges, enhancing self-confidence, and promoting physical healing. It is a holistic tool that taps into the mind's incredible power to manifest positive outcomes.

Incorporating the mind-body connection, meditation, and visualization into your daily routine can significantly enhance your holistic well-being. These practices empower you to take charge of your mental and physical health, paving the way for a life filled with balance, harmony, and fulfillment.

Chapter 9: Holistic Beauty and Self-Confidence

In a world where external beauty standards often take center stage, it's crucial for teenage girls to understand that true beauty emanates from within. This chapter is a journey into holistic beauty, focusing on natural skincare and beauty practices, strategies to boost self-confidence, and the transformative power of body positivity and self-acceptance. Let's explore not only ways to enhance your outer radiance but also to nurture your inner strength.

Natural Skincare and Beauty Practices

Your skin is a reflection of your overall well-being. Embracing natural skincare and beauty practices not only enhances your outer appearance but also nurtures your self-confidence.

Gentle Cleansing: Begin and end your day with a sulfate-free cleanser. This will remove impurities, makeup, and excess oil without stripping your skin of its natural moisture.

Hydration: Keeping your skin hydrated is essential. Apply a chemical-free moisturizer daily to keep your skin supple and prevent dryness.

Sun Protection: Protect your skin from the sun's harmful UV rays by using a natural sunscreen with a suitable SPF rating. Sun protection is a long-term investment in your skin's health and beauty.

Balanced Nutrition: A diet rich in fruits, vegetables, and whole grains, along with proper hydration, can significantly impact your skin's health. Nutrient-dense foods provide essential vitamins and minerals for a radiant complexion.

Mindful Makeup Choices: When choosing makeup products, opt for those free from harmful chemicals. Natural and organic makeup options are widely available and can enhance your beauty without compromising your skin's health.

Stress Management: Stress can negatively affect your skin. Incorporate stress-reduction techniques like meditation, deep breathing, or yoga into your daily routine to keep your skin and mind healthy.

Adequate Sleep: Quality sleep is crucial for healthy skin. Aim for 7-9 hours of uninterrupted sleep to allow your skin to repair and rejuvenate.

Simplicity in Beauty: Less is often more when it comes to skincare. A simplified routine with natural products can allow your true radiance to shine through. Avoid overloading your skin with too many products.

Skin Care Routines and Rituals

Here are some natural skincare routines and rituals to help you maintain a healthy and radiant complexion:

Morning Routine:

Start your day with a gentle cleanse using a sulfate-free facial cleanser.

Apply a chemical-free sunscreen with at least SPF 30 to protect your skin from UV damage.

Use a natural and hydrating moisturizer to keep your skin supple.

A few times a week, exfoliate with a natural scrub to remove dead skin cells gently.

Finish your morning routine with a makeup routine that includes natural and organic products.

Evening Routine:

Remove makeup and cleanse your face with a sulfate-free cleanser to rid your skin of impurities.

Apply a natural, hydrating moisturizer to nourish your skin while you sleep.

For extra pampering, use a natural face mask once a week to revitalize your skin.

Don't forget the importance of quality sleep to rejuvenate your skin.

Weekly Rituals:

Dedicate time to a holistic skincare self-care session once a week. Start with a facial steam to open up your pores.

Follow this with a gentle exfoliation to remove dead skin cells.

Apply a natural face mask tailored to your skin type to provide deep nourishment and relaxation.

Finish your weekly skincare ritual with a calming, hydrating mist.

Natural skincare routines and rituals are not just about the products you use but the care and attention you give to yourself. By dedicating time to nurture your skin, you send a powerful message to yourself that self-care is a priority.

Boosting Self-Confidence

Self-confidence is a vital aspect of holistic well-being. When you feel good about yourself, it radiates outward and enhances your overall beauty.

Positive Self-Talk: Self-confidence begins with positive self-talk. Be your own biggest supporter and practice self-encouragement. Replace self-criticism with self-compassion.

Set Achievable Goals: Establish realistic, attainable goals for yourself. When you achieve them, your confidence will receive a well-deserved boost.

Embrace Failure as Growth: Understand that failure is a stepping stone to success. Embrace it, learn from it, and use it to grow stronger and more self-assured.

Self-Care Rituals: Prioritize self-care to nurture your well-being. Regular self-care rituals can help you feel more confident and resilient.

Positive Body Language: Your body language can influence how you feel about yourself and how others perceive you. Maintain good posture and use open, confident body language to enhance your self-assurance.

Surround Yourself with Positivity: Choose to surround yourself with positive influences and supportive friends who uplift your confidence rather than diminish it.

Celebrate Your Achievements: Celebrate your accomplishments, both big and small. Acknowledging your successes can reinforce your self-worth and boost your self-confidence.

Dress Confidently: Dress in a way that makes you feel confident. Wear clothes that express your personal style and make you feel good about yourself.

Remember that self-confidence is not about striving to conform to society's standards but celebrating your unique radiance and embracing your inner and outer beauty. As you cultivate self-confidence, your authentic beauty will shine brilliantly for all to see.

Chapter 10: Hormonal Changes and Menstrual Health

Adolescence is a time of transformation, not only i
terms of physical and emotional growth but also i
terms of hormonal changes. For teenage girls, thes
hormonal fluctuations can sometimes feel like
rollercoaster ride. This chapter delves into th
understanding of hormonal changes in adolescence
the importance of menstrual health and hygiene, an
offers natural ways to manage PMS and period pain
helping you navigate this crucial aspect of you
holistic well-being.

Understanding Hormonal Changes in Adolescence

Puberty: Puberty is the phase when your body undergoes significant hormonal changes, leading to physical and emotional transformations. During puberty, your body begins producing sex hormones, such as estrogen and progesterone in girls, which trigger the development of secondary sexual characteristics and the onset of menstruation.

Menstrual Cycle: The menstrual cycle is a monthly hormonal dance that prepares your body for the possibility of pregnancy. It involves the release of an egg from the ovaries, thickening of the uterine lining, and the shedding of this lining if pregnancy doesn't occur, resulting in menstruation.

Hormonal Fluctuations: Hormonal fluctuations during the menstrual cycle can affect your mood, energy levels, and physical well-being. Understanding these fluctuations can help you better manage your emotional and physical health throughout your cycle.

Emotional Resilience: As your body adapts to these hormonal changes, you may experience mood swing and emotional ups and downs. Developing emotiona resilience is key to navigating these changes with grace.

Menstrual Health and Hygiene

Hygiene Practices: Maintaining proper hygiene during your menstrual cycle is crucial. Change you menstrual products regularly and keep the genita area clean to prevent infections.

Menstrual Product Options: Explore different menstrual product options, such as pads, tampons menstrual cups, or period panties, to find what works best for you. Consider eco-friendly and sustainable options for a more holistic approach.

Diet and Nutrition: Eating a balanced diet and staying hydrated can support menstrual health. Certain foods can help alleviate symptoms like bloating and mood swings.

Exercise: Regular physical activity can ease menstrual discomfort. Engaging in low-impact exercises, such as yoga or walking, can help alleviate cramps and boost your mood.

Pain Management: If you experience severe menstrual pain, consider natural pain management techniques like heat therapy, herbal teas, or over-the-counter pain relievers. Consult with a healthcare provider for severe pain or irregularities.

Managing PMS and Period Pain Naturally

Nutrition: Incorporate foods rich in calcium, magnesium, and omega-3 fatty acids into your diet to help alleviate PMS symptoms. These nutrients can reduce bloating, mood swings, and cramps.

Herbal Remedies: Herbal remedies like ginger, chamomile, and cinnamon have been known to help relieve menstrual discomfort. Herbal teas or supplements may offer relief.

Heat Therapy: Applying heat to your lower abdomen can relax the uterine muscles and alleviate cramps You can use a hot water bottle or a heated pad for comfort.

Stress Management: Stress can exacerbate PMS symptoms. Engage in stress-reduction techniques such as meditation, deep breathing, or gentle yoga to maintain emotional balance.

Aromatherapy: Essential oils like lavender and clary sage can have calming and pain-relieving properties Use them in a diffuser or diluted in a carrier oil for a soothing massage.

Hydration: Staying well-hydrated is essential fo managing bloating and maintaining overall well-being during your period.

Supportive Lifestyle: Prioritize self-care during your menstrual cycle. Rest, engage in activities that bring you joy, and be kind to yourself.

Understanding your body's hormonal changes, maintaining good menstrual hygiene, and managing PMS and period pain naturally are essential aspects of your holistic well-being. By embracing and caring for your body during this unique phase, you can foster a positive relationship with your menstrual cycle and empower yourself to live a healthier and more balanced life.

Chapter 11: Sleep and Restorative Practices

Sleep is a fundamental component of your holisti well-being. It's during those hours of rest that you body rejuvenates and your mind finds solace. In thi chapter, we will explore the importance of qualit sleep, how to create a sleep-friendly environment and relaxation techniques that can help you achiev better and more restorative sleep.

Importance of Quality Sleep

Sleep is not merely a biological necessity; it's the foundation of a healthy and balanced life. Here's why quality sleep is crucial:

Physical Restoration: Sleep allows your body to repair and regenerate tissues, maintain immune function, and regulate hormones. It's during deep sleep that growth and repair processes are at their peak.

Mental Clarity: Adequate sleep improves cognitive function, memory consolidation, and problem-solving abilities. It enhances your creativity and decision-making.

Emotional Well-Being: Sleep plays a pivotal role in emotional regulation. A lack of sleep can lead to mood swings, irritability, and an increased risk of anxiety and depression.

Physical Health: Consistent, quality sleep is associated with lower risks of chronic diseases such as heart disease, diabetes, and obesity.

Weight Management: Sleep deprivation can disrupt hormones that control appetite and lead to weight gain. Quality sleep supports a healthy metabolism.

Immune System Support: Sleep strengthens you immune system, helping your body defend agains illnesses.

Creating a Sleep-Friendly Environment

Comfortable Mattress and Bedding: Invest in a comfortable mattress and pillows that support your body and sleep style. Your bedding should be inviting and conducive to rest.

Temperature Control: Keep your bedroom at a comfortable temperature. A slightly cooler room is generally more conducive to sleep.

Darkness and Light: Block out excess light with curtains or blinds. If you need a nightlight, opt for one with soft, warm-toned lighting.

Quiet and Noise Control: Minimize noise disruptions by using earplugs or a white noise machine if necessary. A quiet environment is crucial for uninterrupted sleep.

Technology-Free Zone: Avoid screens at least an hour before bedtime. The blue light emitted by phones and tablets can interfere with your body's natural sleep-wake cycle.

Aromatherapy: Consider using calming essential oils like lavender in a diffuser to create a soothing atmosphere in your bedroom.

Organized and Clutter-Free: Keep your bedroom tidy and clutter-free. A clean space promotes relaxation and helps clear your mind.

Relaxation Techniques for Better Sleep

Meditation: Practice relaxation meditation techniques before bed to calm your mind. Focusing on your breath and clearing your thoughts can help ease into a peaceful sleep.

Progressive Muscle Relaxation: This technique involves tensing and then relaxing each muscle group in your body. It can reduce physical tension and promote a sense of relaxation.

Deep Breathing: Deep, slow breaths can signal to your body that it's time to relax. Try inhaling for a count of four, holding for four, and exhaling for four, and repeat until you feel calm.

Yoga and Stretching: Gentle yoga or stretching exercises can relax your body and mind. Certain yoga poses and stretches are specifically designed for better sleep.

Bedtime Routine: Establish a calming bedtime routine that signals to your body that it's time to sleep. This could include reading a book, taking a warm bath, or enjoying a cup of caffeine-free herbal tea.

Guided Imagery: Create a mental sanctuary by using guided imagery. Visualize a peaceful place where you feel safe and relaxed.

Journaling: Write down your thoughts, worries, or to-do lists before bedtime to clear your mind and prevent racing thoughts that can disrupt sleep.

Limit Caffeine and Alcohol: Avoid caffeine and alcohol in the evening, as they can interfere with sleep patterns.

A restful night's sleep is an essential component of your holistic well-being. By prioritizing quality sleep, creating a sleep-friendly environment, and practicing relaxation techniques, you can recharge your body and mind, allowing you to face each day with renewed energy and vitality.

Chapter 12: Staying on Your Holistic Wellness Journey

Congratulations on embarking on this incredible holistic wellness journey! As you reach the final chapter of this book, it's crucial to understand that your wellness path is not a destination but a continuous journey. In this chapter, we'll explore how to stay on your holistic wellness journey by setting goals and tracking progress, overcoming challenges, and connecting with a holistic community for support and inspiration.

Setting Goals and Tracking Progress

Setting goals is the compass that guides your holistic wellness journey. These goals are the stepping stones toward a healthier, more balanced, and fulfilling life.

Define Your Priorities: Start by identifying what aspects of your well-being matter most to you. Is it physical health, emotional resilience, meaningful relationships, or personal growth? Clarifying your priorities will help you set meaningful goals.

SMART Goals: Use the SMART (Specific, Measurable, Achievable, Relevant, Time-Bound) criteria to frame your goals. For example, a SMART goal could be, "I will practice meditation for 10 minutes every day for the next 30 days to reduce stress."

Break It Down: Large goals can be daunting, so break them down into smaller, manageable steps. This makes it easier to track your progress and maintain motivation.

Record Your Goals: Write down your goals in a journal, on your phone, or in a digital planner. Having a record of your goals keeps them at the forefront of your mind.

Track Your Progress: Regularly review your goals and note your progress. Celebrate your successes, and adjust your approach if needed.

Accountability Partner: Share your goals with a friend or family member who can hold you accountable and provide support. You can also join an online wellness group for added accountability.

Stay Flexible: Life can be unpredictable, so be open to adjusting your goals when necessary. Adaptability is a valuable skill on your wellness journey.

Self-Compassion: Be kind to yourself if you encounter setbacks or obstacles. Remember that progress is not always linear, and self-compassion is an essential aspect of holistic well-being.

Overcoming Challenges

On the path to holistic wellness, you may encounter challenges that test your determination and resilience. Here's how to overcome them:

Self-Doubt: Self-doubt can be a significant obstacle. When it arises, remind yourself of your capabilities and the progress you've made. Seek encouragement from friends, mentors, or your holistic community.

Procrastination: Procrastination is a common challenge. Combat it by breaking tasks into smaller steps, setting deadlines, and focusing on the intrinsic rewards of your journey.

Lack of Motivation: Motivation can wane, especially during challenging times. Reconnect with your "why" – the reasons you started your holistic wellness journey. Visualize the benefits you'll reap from your efforts.

Time Management: Balancing various aspects of your well-being can be time-consuming. Create a well-structured daily or weekly schedule that prioritizes your goals and self-care routines.

Stress and Burnout: Wellness journeys can become overwhelming, leading to stress and burnout. Regularly practice stress-relief techniques and be open to seeking professional help when needed.

Negativity and Self-Criticism: Negative self-talk and self-criticism can hold you back. Cultivate self-compassion and replace negative thoughts with affirmations that reinforce your worth.

Social Pressures: Peer pressure or societal expectations can deter you from your path. Stay true to your values and goals, and surround yourself with a supportive community.

Balance: Balancing different aspects of holistic wellness can be a challenge. Prioritize your wellness journey and consider seeking guidance from wellness experts or mentors.

Connecting with a Holistic Community

You don't have to walk this journey alone. Connecting with a holistic community can provide you with support, inspiration, and a sense of belonging. Here's how to connect with like-minded individuals:

Online Forums and Social Media: There are many online wellness communities, forums, and social media groups where you can connect with people who share your goals. Engage in discussions, ask questions, and offer your insights.

Wellness Retreats and Workshops: Consider attending wellness retreats or workshops to immerse yourself in a holistic environment. These events can be both educational and transformative.

Local Wellness Groups: Seek out local wellnes groups or meetups in your area. Connecting with people face-to-face can foster deeper connections.

Mentors and Coaches: A wellness mentor or coach can provide personalized guidance, motivation, and accountability.

Accountability Partners: Partner with a friend or family member who shares your wellness goals. Regular check-ins can help keep you both on track.

Volunteer Opportunities: Many wellness communities offer volunteer opportunities. Getting involved in wellness-related causes can be a fulfilling way to connect with others who are passionate about holistic well-being.

Sharing Your Journey: Don't be afraid to share your wellness journey with others. Your experiences, successes, and challenges can inspire and support those on a similar path.

Your holistic wellness journey is a lifelong adventure that will lead you to greater self-awareness, balance, and fulfillment. Remember that every step, no matter how small, contributes to your overall well-being. As you set and track your goals, overcome challenges, and connect with a holistic community, you'll find that this journey is not just about reaching a destination but about embracing the ever-evolving process of becoming your best self.

Conclusion: Blossoming Naturally

In closing, "Blossom Naturally: The Teenage Girl's Holistic Wellness Handbook" has been a heartfelt journey through the realms of holistic well-being, self-discovery, and personal growth. As we reach the final chapter, I want to express my gratitude for joining me on this path.

Throughout this book, we've delved into the various aspects of well-being, from understanding your emotional self to nurturing your body, mind, and spirit. We've explored natural skincare, self-confidence, and the intricacies of managing hormonal changes.

The journey of holistic wellness is not just a chapter in a book, but a lifelong pursuit. It's about embracing self-acceptance, building resilience, and living a life filled with vitality and joy.

As you close this book, remember that your wellness journey is uniquely yours. Continue setting goals, tracking progress, overcoming challenges, and connecting with like-minded individuals. You are a remarkable, strong, and beautiful individual, and your journey toward holistic well-being has only just begun.

May you find the wisdom, strength, and confidence to blossom naturally, radiating your true beauty from the inside out. Your well-being is a precious gift, and you are deserving of a life filled with holistic health, self-love, and happiness. Thank you for being a part of this journey, and may your path be filled with light, love, and endless growth.

Milton Keynes UK
Ingram Content Group UK Ltd.
UKHW020926201123
432908UK00021B/3170